Text and Illustrations Copyright © 2017 by
Dr. Felicia Williams McGowan

.

Address all inquiries to: Dr. Felicia Williams McGowan

Email: **drwilliamsmcgowan@gmail.com**

Dedication

This journal is dedicated to the journey that took place during the Spring season when Hattie reviewed her goals. During this time of the year Hattie begin to see if she was on the right lane to success.

This Journal Belongs To

_____

Date:

Keep traveling through your journey

Date: _____

_____
_____
_____
_____
_____
_____
_____
_____
_____
_____
_____
_____
_____
_____
_____
_____
_____
_____
_____
_____
_____
_____
_____
_____
_____

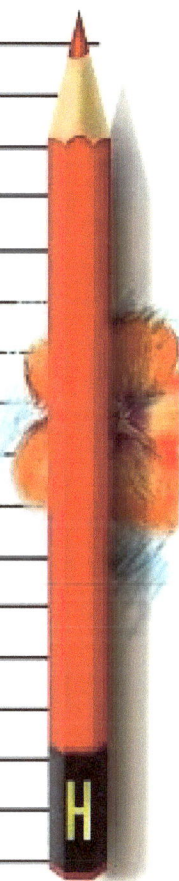

Keep traveling through your journey

Date: _____

_____
_____
_____
_____
_____
_____
_____
_____
_____
_____
_____
_____
_____
_____
_____
_____
_____
_____
_____
_____
_____
_____
_____
_____
_____
_____

Keep traveling through your journey

Date: _____

Keep traveling through your journey

Date:

Keep traveling through your journey

Date:
_____

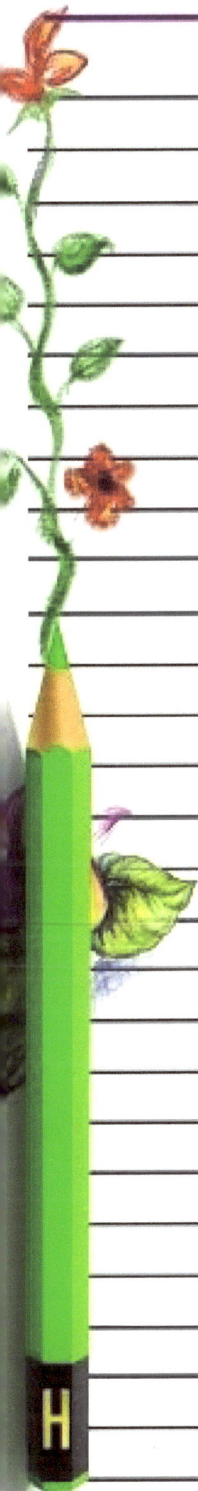

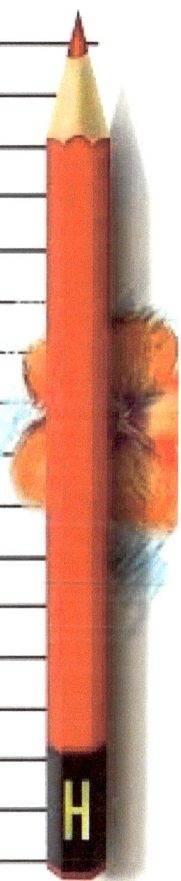

Keep traveling through your journey

Date:

Keep traveling through your journey

Date:

Keep traveling through your journey

Date:
_____

_____

_____

_____

_____

_____

_____

_____

_____

_____

_____

_____

_____

_____

_____

_____

_____

_____

_____

_____

_____

_____

_____

_____

_____

_____

Keep traveling through your journey

Date:

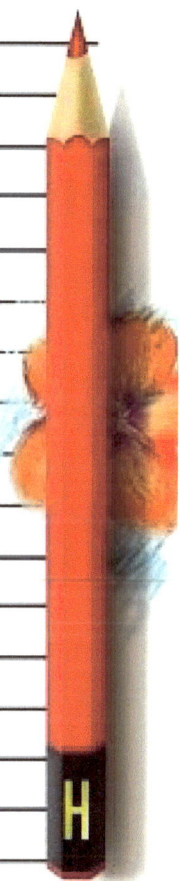

Keep traveling through your journey

Date: _____

_____
_____
_____
_____
_____
_____
_____
_____
_____
_____
_____
_____
_____
_____
_____
_____
_____
_____
_____
_____
_____
_____

Keep traveling through your journey

Date:

Keep traveling through your journey

Date:

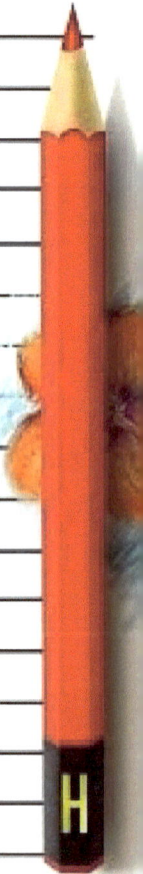

Keep traveling through your journey

Date: _____

_____
_____
_____
_____
_____
_____
_____
_____
_____
_____
_____
_____
_____
_____
_____
_____
_____
_____
_____
_____
_____
_____
_____
_____

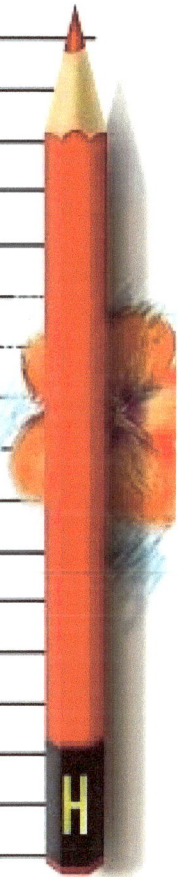

Keep traveling through your journey

Date: _____

_____
_____
_____
_____
_____
_____
_____
_____
_____
_____
_____
_____
_____
_____
_____
_____
_____
_____
_____
_____
_____
_____
_____

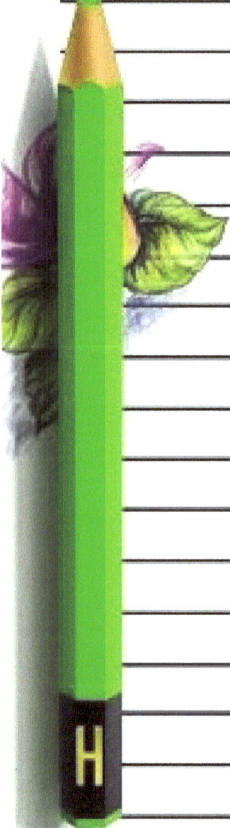

Keep traveling through your journey

Date: _____

Keep traveling through your journey

Date:

Keep traveling through your journey

Date: _____

_____
_____
_____
_____
_____
_____
_____
_____
_____
_____
_____
_____
_____
_____
_____
_____
_____
_____
_____
_____
_____
_____

Keep traveling through your journey

Date:

Keep traveling through your journey

Date:

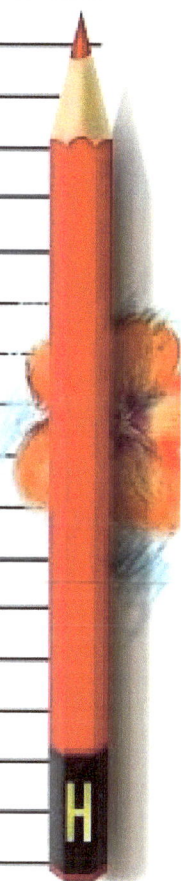

Keep traveling through your journey

Date:

Keep traveling through your journey

Date:

Keep traveling through your journey

Date: _____

Keep traveling through your journey

Date: _____

Keep traveling through your journey

Date: _____

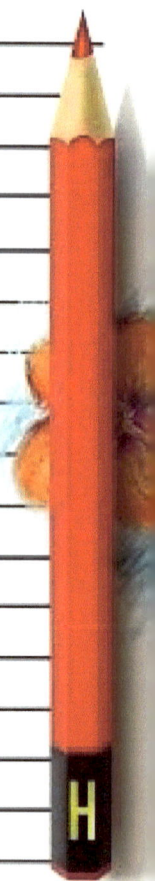

Keep traveling through your journey

Date:

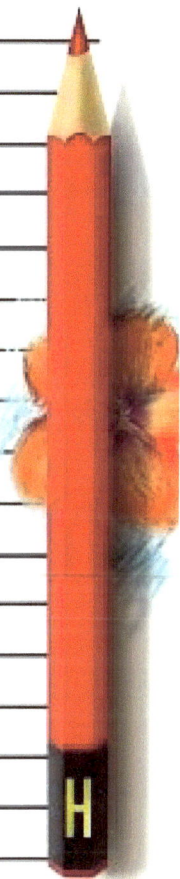

Keep traveling through your journey

Date: _____

_____
_____
_____
_____
_____
_____
_____
_____
_____
_____
_____
_____
_____
_____
_____
_____
_____
_____
_____
_____
_____
_____
_____
_____

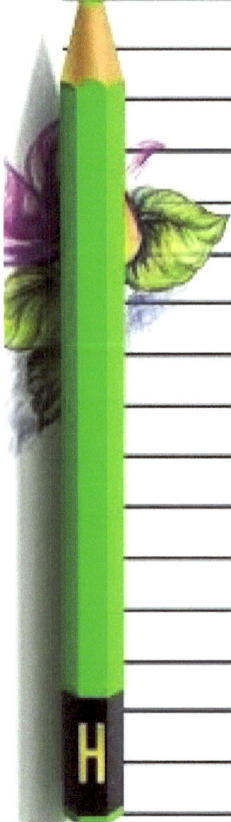

Keep traveling through your journey

Date: _____

Keep traveling through your journey

Date:

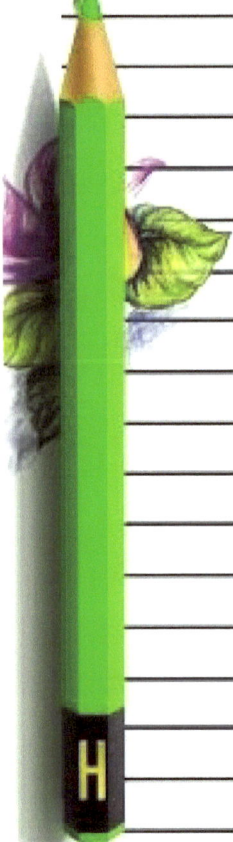

Keep traveling through your journey

Date:

Keep traveling through your journey

Date:

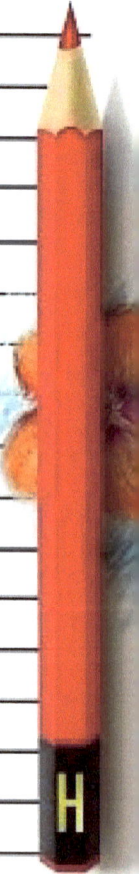

Keep traveling through your journey

Get What You Deserve

What is your dream house, where would you like to live and why? Explain what type of siding you would brick, wood, etc, how many bedrooms, bathroom, whether you want to live on the ranch or city. Be very detailed in your description of your house.

_____
_____
_____
_____
_____
_____
_____
_____
_____
_____
_____
_____
_____
_____
_____
_____
_____
_____
_____
_____
_____
_____
_____

Keep traveling through your journey

Date: _____

A Picture of My Dream Home

Draw a picture that represents your dream house using the details listed on the previous page using street signs, business, etc of where you dream of residing one day.

Keep traveling through your journey

Using Math Skills

Math is an essential part of school. You will need math for the rest of your life whether you are adding, subtracting, or measuring things. Complete the math problems below.

If you worked for 7 days earning 2.50 a day and on the 7th day you paid for 50 for gum and 2.00 for a hamburger. How much would you have left?

Hattie dreamed of being nurse one day to help people with kidney disease like her. If Hattie had earned $729 in two weeks, but paid $350 in rent and $129 in groceries. How much money Hattie would have left after 4 weeks?

Keep traveling through your journey

Date: _____

Spring Journal Word Search

Word List

****

```
M O S P Z M J I H X S M H W D E U
A R P A G I A L I K E S N W C F V
Y D I S L I K E S F F N C N M Z M
X P I Q Z G J G V K N D W I B A E
Q G K H B H Y Z L E K F N T H E V
P Z O C G A P Z W L L X T A S T Q
H I T P T N E M E V E I H C A W Z
T Y Z L P W P J S Z S A R X Z L Y
Z W F X H O Y E R X M V V G A E Z
F M J A F D R U C B A W M X S J D
M B B S F U Q T N W E O E F K Y Y
A E L D U V K P U P R L X D W M H
A J G K L P E K G N D H C B K Z H
E H B V E R P O V P I R M H F S C
R L E V A R A O I P Z T N S U B L
N E E F M L B K R V A D Y A R O M
O C W P S H D O Y T T A A N B J C
```

****

Achievement	Support	Opportunity
Dislikes	Likes	Dreams
Jobs	Goals	

Keep traveling through your journey

Find Other Books About Hattie And Her Amazing Journey at Amazon.com

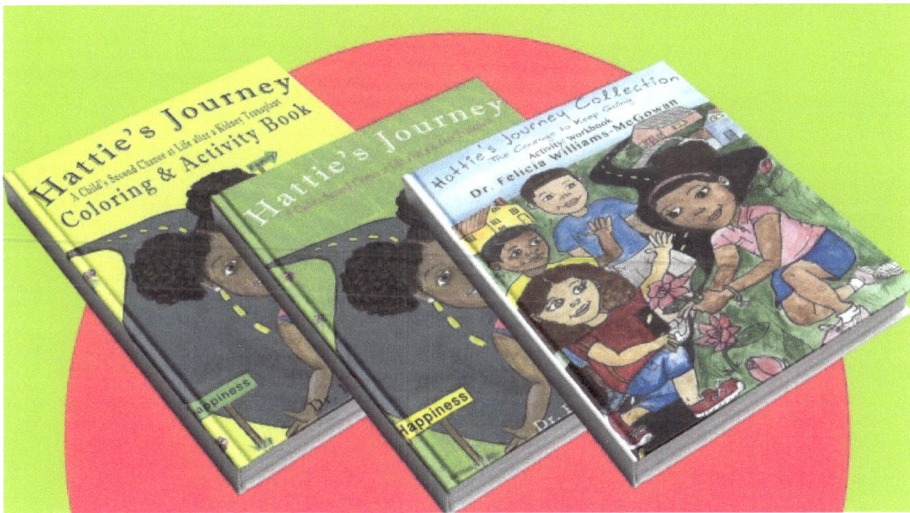

www.ingramcontent.com/pod-product-compliance
Lightning Source LLC
LaVergne TN
LVHW072055070426
835508LV00002B/115